Understanding SEO

A Comprehensive Guide

By Aram Karapetyan

Owner and President of Website Design By Adam (WDBA).

Table of Contents

Introduction...

Part 1: Keyword Research

    Chap. 1: Keyword Basics

    Chap. 2: Target Market Research: Keyword/Phrase Generation

    Chap. 3: Keyword Analysis and Competitor Assessment

    Chap 4: SEO Strategy: Long Tail to Broad Head

Part 2: On-Page Optimization

    Chap. 5: Website Architecture

    Chap. 6: Website Coding

    Chap. 7: Content Optimization

Part 3: Site Promotion (Off-Page Optimization)

    Chap. 8: Understanding the Importance of Link-Building

    Chap. 9: Link Building 101

Conclusion

Introduction

If you are reading this book, it is likely that either you or your webmaster recently launched a website for your business. Now, however, you are wondering, "Why can't I find my website when I search for it on Google? It is as if the site is invisible!" You need not worry. This response is one of the most common reactions entrepreneurs have just after their sites launch.

So why are the search engines avoiding your site?

The short answer is that the search engines will largely continue to ignore your site until it is made search engine friendly and marketed. Right now the search engines cannot even see your site because you are not speaking their language. In addition, because the search engines cannot detect your site, no one else can either, and this makes it even worse because without visitors and without links to other sites, there are few opportunities for improving your internet profile.

So how do you teach your site to speak the language of the search engines and start getting some traffic?

The answer is summarized in three deceivingly simple sounding letters, S E O.

SEO, Search Engine Optimization, is the process by which you make your site visible to search engines through a complicated mix of site restructuring and web marketing. Without SEO, your website has little to no chance as far as the search engines are concerned. SEO is what will get you the exposure your business needs to succeed in a marketplace increasingly driven by those with the most prominent web presence. As the internet landscape has become more complicated and intertwined with the global marketplace, web marketers have sharpened their SEO skills and learned through years of trial and research how to deliver their clients' websites right to where their customers live. Part science, part art, and part hard-earned experience, the craft of SEO has become the art of giving customers what they want, when they want it, so that you make the sale. It's the know-how that affords your site the best opportunity to increase its organic search engine ranking so that it can break into that all important top 20 search results for your chosen keywords—instead of page 20, where your site will gather dust instead of clicks.

How will this book help you? The purpose of this book is to acquaint you with the SEO process so that you can come to a more practical understanding of what it will take for your website to succeed in attracting visitors who are ready to become customers. The book is divided into three parts:

Part 1: Keyword Research: This part will give you an overview of how keywords and phrases work within search and explain how keywords are chosen for SEO.

Part 2: On-Page Optimization: In this part, you will learn how your website must be written and structured in order to allow search engines to find it and index it properly.

Part 3: Site Promotion: In the final section, you will learn what off-page steps you and your SEO marketing team must take in order to help your site's ranking to improve. This section explains everything from how to get links from other sites to how to use social marketing to increase your site's effectiveness.

When you have completed this e-book, I hope that you will have enough information that you could attempt to execute your own SEO campaign, if you had the time or inclination. However, I should warn you that SEO is not a casual practice that you can successfully dally at for a couple of hours every other weekend. If you are serious about getting your site to rank well and to attract visitors ready to convert, you should leave this up to experienced professionals.

Part 1: Keyword Research

Chapter One: Keyword Basics

Keywords or, more accurately keywords and keyword phrases, are the terms that people use to perform searches on the Internet. When you type a search such as "New York Style Pizza" into the internet, you are using keywords to look for information. Before Google came on the scene and revolutionized search this process was much more limited and, as you probably remember, a person looking for something would have to struggle to key the right terms into the search engine of choice. Even then, many of the responses you would get back would be website spam—sites that were high on advertisements for products but low on actual information. Now, however, just about any word that you put in will retrieve a number of relevant choices. Everyday, of course, thousands of new phrases are searched for and many of them will become tomorrow's keyword phrases.

This much you probably already know. So how do Google and the other search engines find the answers to these millions of individual queries? Once you type in your search, Google scours its index for pages about those keywords. Occasionally you might search for something for which there are only fleeting references, but more often than not, the problem for the search engine is to sort through thousands, perhaps millions of possible results. A keyword phrase like "New York style pizza" is exactly that kind of keyword phrase. Just imagine the number of internet pages that have the words "New York" on them, or "pizza".

So how does the Google algorithm decide which pages to display on the first page of your search results? In order to determine which pages will be most useful for you, Google looks to a number of criteria from the way the page is tagged in its HTML code to whether the links on the page are active. One of the main criteria is whether the keyword phrase appears on the web page and where it is placed. As you might expect, if the keyword phrase appears in the title or subtitles (and is tagged appropriately), Google ranks this page higher than when it does not since Google is looking for pages that directly answer your query. In addition, Google will look at how often the word appears on the page, on the theory that pages that discuss the keyword phrase throughout will be more relevant than those that do not.

This, of course, is where SEO comes in. SEO looks to format pages (including their underlying HTML tags) in such a way that search engines will be able to see the keyword relevancy more clearly and thus rank the individual pages higher than they might otherwise be placed without clarification.

The problem for websites is that with so many companies optimizing their sites, being able to cut through the noise to the first page of Google search returns is no easy task. Nor can the importance of ranking high be understated. Studies show that the farther down the list your page appears on search results, the less likely you are to have customers click on your link. In fact, rarely do internet users go beyond the third Search Engine Results Page (abbreviated with the acronym SERP).

This means then, that in order to be visible, you must get your website to rank among the top 30 listings (the first three SERPs) and preferably within the top ten (the first SERP). If you end up on page 20, you might as well not be there at all since the likelihood of anyone seeing your site is extremely small. Of course, with so many sites creating pages for SEO, Google still has to have other criteria to organize search results. So, in addition, to keywords, Google also considers the relative strength of the web page and the site on which it is displayed. More established sites, with good traffic, and multiple links from other similarly themed sites and pages that also have a good ranking on Google search results are given priority over sites and pages that have recently come into existence, have few visits, and/or have no quality links. Google calls this ranking system PageRank—a play off Google founder Larry Page's name, in part—and although having your site keyword optimized is the number one criteria in placing high on SERPs, PageRank works as a sort of tiebreaker between equally well-optimized pages, with the higher PageRanked site getting the call in close cases. Thus Wikipedia will tend to beat out JoesParrotFacts.com on a search for "Amazon Parrots."

Let's be clear, however, PageRank only works as a kind of tiebreaker. Regardless of whether I have a PageRank of 1 or 8, if my webpage is not keyword optimized for a particular keyword phrase, I will not rank well in it. So, for example, if I keyword optimize my PageRank 1 site for the search term "little red wheelbarrow" and a rival PageRank 8 website does not, my site will beat out the rival site on the SERPs because mine will simply seem more relevant for that search query than that my rival's website does. For this reason, finding the right keywords is all important to a successful SEO strategy.

(If you are interested in seeing the ranking of pages you visit, you can download the Google toolbar and put the PageRank scale right at the top. You will notice that Google gets the highest rating of 10 with the bar being completely full, while most sites you visit are lucky if they can get a 5 or 6. The website, Alexa.com, a site that monitors and analyzes internet traffic, also has a similar rank display tool, but many internet professionals and security programs consider it to be spyware because it tracks your movements and reports them back to Alexa.)

Given what I have written so far about the way Google and other search engines create their search returns, you can probably see the problem this kind of ranking system creates for your new site. If you have a new website, you are unlikely to be getting a lot of traffic or have a number of great in bound links yet, so you are at an automatic disadvantage in relation to your more established competitors.

In order for your web pages to challenge the pages of your competitors, it will take a determined effort and it will take time. Your site will not suddenly jump to the top of all your most coveted keywords within a week. Before you even get started, you will have to set up a well-thought out SEO strategy that targets your audience through their natural search patterns. The key to this strategy is to create a list of keywords/phrases that draws in conversion ready visitors. Creating this list is what we will turn to next.

Chapter 2: Target Market Research

Creating Your First Keyword List: Now that you have a sense of how keywords work and how this is important for your website, it is time to start thinking about which keywords you will want to include on your keyword list. This might seem obvious at first. If you own a real estate company in Pasadena, for example, you might want to have "Pasadena Real Estate," "Historic Pasadena Homes," "California Bungalow Style Homes" and "Homes Near Los Angeles" all as your keywords.

If you have a consultant, you may be tempted to simply let her come up with your list. In this early stage, however, you will be much better served by taking the time to generate most of this initial list on your own. Although SEO marketing consultants can be vital to success of an SEO campaign, they do not have the amount of experience in your field that you do, and this experience will be vitally important in creating a list that suits your needs.

Brainstorming a Longer List: You should probably be able to come up with a dozen to two dozen such phrases without much difficulty. You will want to keep going however. You want to get as big a list as possible, because you want to have a large pool from which to select your main keywords. Look to combine words from separate phrases and change the order. Remember that order matters in searches. So "Historic Pasadena Real Estate" will yield different results on search engines than "Historic Real Estate in Pasadena."

Here are some other variations to consider as you fill out your list:

- Brand Names: If you offer a Brand name item that people may know well enough to search for by name that should definitely be on your list. Once a web user has narrowed their search terms to brand names, they are often ready to buy.
- Location Terms: If your business is specific to an area, it is often useful to include your location and those nearby so that your place can be more easily found by locals searching the web.

- Hyphenated Words: Some phrases use hyphens and some do not, so be sure to include both hyphenated and unhyphenated words.

- Alternate Spellings: Although the Google Algorithm will penalize your site for misspellings, it may be helpful to look for alternate spellings of words in American versus British English. If the word "jewelry," for example, has a higher level of competition than the word "jewellery" (the British spelling), than you may want to use the British spelling. Be careful, however, that you do not annoy customers by switching between the two spellings so much that you make discerning customers question your attention to detail and professionalism. (Acronyms and abbreviations work similarly, so don't forget to consider them as well: LA vs. Los Angeles, Cal versus UC Berkeley.)

- Plurals: Include not only the singular but the plural version of words. Search engines recognize these as separate. Thus, "pizza" and "pizzas" will bring somewhat separate results during searches

- Synonyms: Try a thesaurus and think of other words that have similar meanings that could work just as well.

Using Keyword Tools: You should not solely rely on your own cognitive abilities for generating your keyword list. In addition to sharing your list with as many of your colleagues as possible to see if they have any new ideas, you can also use some online tools to help generate new keyword ideas.

The Google Keyword Tool: Google, Word Tracker, and other SEO Marketing sites all have keyword generation and analysis tools that can help you fill out your list. Google's Keyword Tool has the advantage of being free (as long as you have a Google login). It will take your list and generate hundreds of related phrases from it. In addition to suggesting phrases Google will also give you access to quite a bit of vital search information that will come in handy later on as you begin to narrow and refine your list. For example, when you look at the list the Google Keyword Tool has generated you will see a column that tells you how often people search for each term or phrase on Google. This will give you a good sense as to the level of interest in that particular phrase and will help you to determine whether this phrase should be part of your final target list. (For now, however, we are only looking to expand the list, not yet to narrow it to target keywords.)

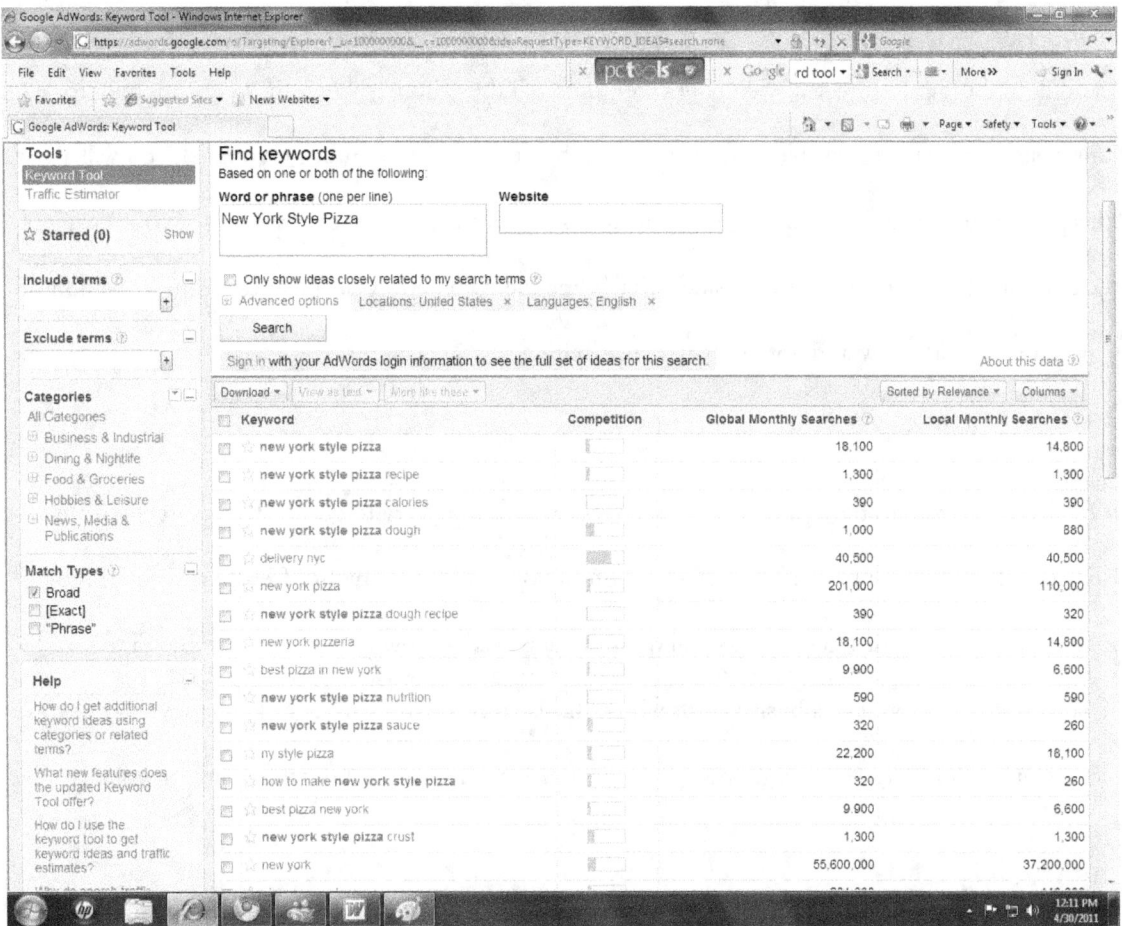

Data-Mining your Customers: The key to good SEO is knowing your customers. That means that you have to get a good sense of not only what your customers want but about how your customers think about what they want. This is not always the easiest intellectual activity to accomplish. As we get used to working in our industries, we begin to forget how outsiders view what we do. For example, a real estate broker may be very fluent in the language of home types and know exactly what a Tudor style home is versus a Mediterranean, while the majority of us may only have the vaguest notions or even be mislead by such descriptions. A potential customer may like a particular type of home but not have the language with which to search for it. They may write "southwest style homes" because they associate Ranch homes or Mission Style homes with California and Arizona, but may not be able to get any more specific.

This is important for SEO because if you optimize your site for "Mission Style Homes" or "Ranch style homes" and don't bother to find out what your customers call these homes when they are searching for them, your customers may not be able to find you. For this reason when you begin your list, you will always want to keep your customers in mind. Even as you are listing all the possible descriptors for your business that you can think of, you also want to consider what someone coming to your business from a position of relative ignorance would know and not know when searching.

Customer Feedback: In order to flesh out your list even more, you should try to get feedback directly from your customers. If you own a brick and mortar version of your store, you might offer them a coupon or entry into a prize giveaway for filling out a small questionnaire asking how they might search online for what you sell. If you do not have a business for which this is convenient, you might have to wait until you get customers online and then encourage them to give you a clearer sense of how they think of your business.

Chap. 3: Keyword Analysis and Competitor Assessment

Goal Setting: Once you have created a substantial list that gives you the greatest amount of flexibility, you want to start thinking about how you will narrow and refine this list so that it focuses on a powerful set of keyword phrases that will deliver your customers to you. Your criteria for determining which keywords to use will have a lot to do with your goals. Of course, generally speaking the goal of SEO is to increase the amount of traffic and page views you get in order to increase your *conversion rate*—the percentage of visitors to your page (or site) that perform the action you have designed your page to achieve (e.g., signing up for a your site's newsletter, or buying the e-book associated with the page). Put differently, you are not just trying to get a lot of visitors to your site, but to increase the number of visitors who are looking for what you are promoting.

The point here is that not all traffic is equal. If you own a real estate site in Pasadena, for example, you aren't just looking for heavy traffic to your website. You want to increase the number of visitors that are looking to buy a home in Pasadena. For this reason your website might include not only posts having to do with Pasadena homes but also postings about Pasadena's public schools, Pasadena crime rates, maybe even commute times. In part, you are trying to build a relationship of trust with people who are researching places to live so that if they decide to move they will give your business a try.

On the other hand, if you have a website about "Historic Pasadena Homes" and you have a book on this topic that you are trying to sell, your posts might have more to do with the historic Pasadena neighborhoods than with the current state of the school system. You might, for example, include an article about "Pasadena history," an article about "Los Angeles historic homes" or a page about "Los Angeles history books."

Now, in the examples above there might be some cross-over between the two groups. In other words, there may be some internet users who could be both interested in buying a home in Pasadena and in buying a book about Pasadena's historic homes, but, for the most part, these groups will not overlap. Your campaign goal will determine how you narrow your list and which segment of searchers you target.

Tracking Competitor Strategies: In addition to creating your own list of relevant keywords, it is a good idea to take a look at your main competitors' strategies. For example, if you are that Pasadena real estate broker, it might benefit you to take a look at the other Pasadena realtors that do well on web-searches and to examine what keywords they are using and how. As you learn more about SEO, you will often be able to pick out the main keywords they are using by just looking at the title and first line of each page and picking out the keywords that repeat.

The Google Keyword Tool is useful here again. You can simply put your competitor's URL into the search box and you will get a list of the keywords that Google recognizes on the website's pages. There are also a number of other search devices on the internet that will perform a similar service, but the Google Keyword Tool is free.

If you want to look more closely at the HTML of a particular page, you can take a look at your competitor's source code by clicking on the view tab on your browser and finding the View Source option. This will reveal the architecture of the page. Often you can find the keywords listed on the tag line that reads <META NAME= "*keywords*">. Looking over your competitors' keywords will not only help you fill out your own keyword list but often will help you to see what strategy they are using so that you can co-opt the more successful aspects of this strategy.

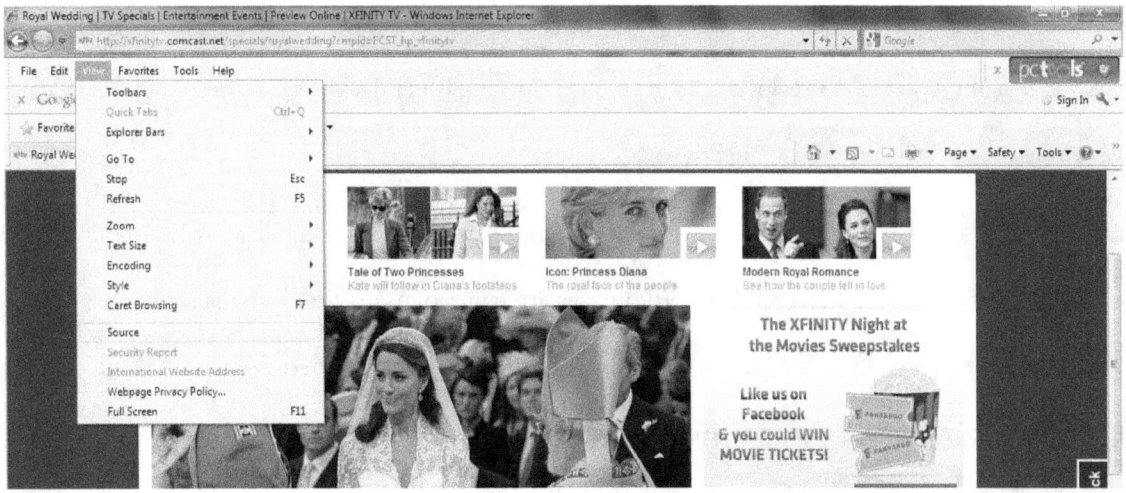

Keyword Analysis: Once you have generated your list you will want to determine which keywords you want to use. The Google Keyword Tool or similar keyword tools like those offered by Word Tracker will be helpful here. By comparing the number of searches that a keyword phrase generates to the amount of competition for these keywords, you can come to some sense of how easily your page will be able to rank for that keyword search.

Broad Head and *Long Tail:* Keyword analysis will reveal the distinction between "broad head" and "long tail" searches. The basic idea is fairly simple. There are some searches that everyone searches for at first in a given category. So, for example, if I am interested in making a pizza and am searching for a recipe, I might start by typing in "pizza" into the search engine. This is a "broad head" search keyword (a keyword that will always get a heavy number of searches because it is such a catch all). The problem for searchers with a broad head search is that the majority of the results the searcher gets will probably not fit what the searcher is looking for. So, for example, because "pizza" is a highly competitive keyword and because everyone from pizzerias to Italian recipe books will want to rank high for it, a good portion of the results will not fit exactly what I am looking for.

As customers continue to search, however, they will begin to make their searches more specific. So on a second search I might write "pizza recipes" and get a more specific list and as I read more I might decide that I want "New York style pizza with anchovies."

These more specific searches that get somewhat less traffic but that are super specific, are what are known as "long tail" keyword phrases. Long tail keyword phrases are favored in SEO for two main reasons: First, the competition tends to be lower in many long tail keyword phrases. That is, there will be fewer sites that have SEO'd pages to match these long tail searches. This means that if you create a page specifically targeted to this kind of long tail search, you are far more likely to rank in the top 20 search results. You may even be able to get in the highly favored top three organic results.

Second, customers tend to use long tail keyword phrases near the end of the searching process when they have roughly decided what they want and are just looking for a place to get that item. This is because of the process we outlined above. Broad head searches tend to be vague, exploratory searches when customers are just beginning to think about what they want, but as the search process continues, customers begin to refine their searches and to define what they want. For this reason, if you can get a customer to your site at the end of his or her search, it is far easier to make a conversion.

Chap 4: Creating an SEO Strategy that Works for Your Business

Fine Tuning your Keyword List: Now that you have your monster list of possible keywords, your next step will be to narrow and refine this list down to the actual set of keywords you will use to optimize your website. In order to do this you will have to set up an SEO strategy that best fits your business. You want to pick a mix of keywords that has the best chance of getting customers to your site that are likely to make conversions.

For a website that is just starting out, the strategy will usually be one of going from long tail keyword phrases in order to work towards broad head keywords. The reasoning is that as a new site you are unlikely to be able to compete with the established companies that fight for the central broad head searches. In addition, it may not even be in your interest to compete for these terms since you may simply be trying to establish yourself in a niche market. Thus, if we look back to the previous example, if the central goal of your website is to sell a pizza recipe book, then you might not need to rank high for the broad head search term "recipe book," where you will compete with all kinds of recipe books from Italian cuisines to Peruvian, from hamburgers to caviar. Even "Italian recipe book" or "pizza recipe book" might be highly competitive broad head search terms for this category, though you will likely want to add one or both of these for some of your pages. In fact, your best strategy might be trying to rank high for long tail terms like "New York style pizza recipe" or "authentic Sicilian pizza" or "exotic pizza recipes." These more specific long tail search phrases are likely to have fewer global searches but are more likely to deliver site visitors ready to buy your recipe book. This will let you start increasing your profits more quickly.

Of course, your SEO strategy also needs to think long term. This is why you also want to include some terms that are either broad head or at least close to broad head terms. Especially if you can find some terms that have lower competition. As your site's traffic begins to grow and get more attention, these slightly broader terms will draw more visitors as they climb in the rankings, which will, in turn, help your site's reputation to increase and further rise in rankings as well.

Now I do not want to give you the impression that once you have decided on your list you can set up your SEO and let your site run on auto-pilot. SEO, like all forms of marketing, requires continued attention. As your site grows and develops and as the internet landscape adopts new technologies and cultural practices, you will have to continue to adapt your site to match and capitalize on these changes. In addition, search engines also consider changing sites as more relevant than static. New content is a must for sites that want to remain relevant on the internet.

Part 2: On-Page Optimization

Chapter One: Website Architecture

The core of Search Engine Optimization is On-Page Optimization. We can roughly divide this part of SEO into three sections: the optimization of the website architecture, the placement of keywords into the underlying coding and the creation of keyword focused content for your site. We will go over each of these aspects of On-Site Optimization in the three chapters that make up this part.

In this first section, concerning website architecture, I will detail how you can structure your website so that it will help search engines and users read it more easily. Before I begin this section, however, I want to clarify the goal of On-Page Optimization. On-Page Optimization aims to improve your site's visibility by making it more readable for *both* search engines and visitors. This dual goal of On-Page Optimization is what can make it problematic at times. For example, as we will see in the section having to do with content, often what makes for good, creative writing is not what makes for clear SEO. Although the stated purpose of search engines like Google is to deliver relevant web-pages to web users, the creation of web pages that appeal to search engines is not always completely aligned with the pages that users prefer. So as we go through this part, we will often find ourselves discussing how aspects of web page design that may be appealing to those authoring the page are not always the best practices when it comes to getting high SERP position.

I do not want however, to over-emphasize this tension. Many of the guidelines for getting your page indexed properly are also practices that users prefer. It is easy when we are first designing our pages to get carried away with the fancy bells and whistles of web design and forget that the primary emphasis should be on making our pages *practical* and *easy to use*. Attractive graphics and colorful language are nice embellishments, but we should not emphasize them to the detriment of site effectiveness.

So, what can you do to make your site more readable to both search engines and your target web audience?

Choose a Search Friendly URL

One of the earliest and most important decisions you make is deciding on a URL. (A URL is a Universal {or Uniform} Resource Locator. It is the core web address for your site.) You may be tempted simply to use your name or your company's name as the URL. This is a good idea for a company with a strong brand presence, but could be a mistake for a company that is just starting out. Just like your keywords, you want to have a URL that people can find with as little effort as possible. Take our pizza recipe book example from the previous part: you would much rather have "pizzabook.com" than "joepaillaiaztzi.com." (Unless, of course, Joe Paillaiaztizi was a famous enough chef that he would draw traffic. Though, even then, the difficulty of spelling that name would cause problems.)

What are some of the characteristics of a good URL?

- *Make the URL Clear and Descriptive:* Ideally, a web user should be able to figure out what your site is all about by just looking at the address. When possible, put the central focus of your website right in the URL.

- *Place One of your Main Keywords in the Address:* Some of the best web addresses contain one of the central keywords or keyword phrases related to the website's content. So "pizzabook.com" would work well because it contains both the word "pizza" and "book" and since search engines give extra weight to websites that contain users' search terms in their URL, this is, in itself, a good SEO strategy.

- *Avoid Unusual Spellings and Unnecessary Punctuation:* We are sometimes tempted to include some kind of unusual spelling as a sort of pun in order to emphasize some aspect of our website or to just be playful. These kinds of odd variations will inevitably cause searchers problems finding your site. Similarly, avoid putting dashes into your website unless you must, and if you do have to use a dash, try to limit it to only one.

- *Use ".com" when possible:* There are a number of options for your top level domain name (a *top level domain name* is the suffix for your domain name—for example, ".com," ".org," ".net" or ".gov"). Unless you have a very good reason for using one of the alternatives, you want to stick with ".com" since it is the default web suffix that everyone expects. (An exception to this might be if you have a website that reviews television shows, for example, when you might use the ".tv" suffix for extra emphasis. Or, if you have a non-profit organization and want to make sure that visitors don't believe that you are exploiting your particular charity, you might include the ".org" as an extra assurance that you are an organization and not a commercial, for profit, site.

Hosting Requirements: There are also some important qualities you want to look for in the company that hosts your website. Be sure that you are allowed to place as many web pages as you would like on the website and that you have full control over how you place your pages. You want to be able to have direct access to the HTML code so that you can take full advantage of all SEO practices. There are a number of low cost hosting companies that will give you what you want for a reasonable price so be sure to shop around before deciding on your company.

Optimize Graphics

You can also take a number of actions to make your web pages more search engine friendly even once you have created your site. Here are some of the most prominent considerations:

- *Eliminate Flash:* Many sites like to start you off with a fancy Flash display right from the landing page. (A landing page is the first page visitors find when they come to your site from either a SERP result or from an ad. The *landing page* is the equivalent of the first impression.) Flash does offer some pretty attractive possibilities, but it is a bad idea on two counts. First, a lot of web surfers will simply just click right back off your page when they come across this kind of an introductory graphic. Because Flash is so demanding when it comes to computer resources, it will also cause many computers to freeze up as they load, and thus cause visitors to x out of your page. More often than not, these visitors will not return. Second, web crawlers also have a problem with Flash, and they too will often just turn back and leave your page un-indexed when they find Flash at your site's entrance. (A web crawler is the program that search engines like Google send out to survey the web and gather summaries and copies of all the pages contained therein. If your page doesn't get indexed, it is invisible to search engines like Google.) The simplest solution to this problem is just to avoid using Flash and if you do really want to use it, use it sparingly and not as your site's first impression.

- *Image Compression:* For the same reasons that you should avoid Flash, you should employ image compression. This is especially important if you are using Javascript or if you have a lot images on your site (for example, if you have an image carousel). Most users are okay with waiting a few seconds for one picture to load, but not okay with waiting a few seconds when each of 30 images load. Image compression helps speed this load process.

- *Careful with Cookies:* Although it is okay to have cookies on your page, you want to make sure that you do not have cookies that visitors must accept in order to have access to your site. If you don't disable this aspect of your cookies, not only will you drive away a segment of web surfers who simply don't like having cookies placed on their computers, but you will also turn search bots away which are not capable of accepting cookies, thus leaving your page un-indexed.

- *Avoid Dynamic Pages for Keyword Placement:* Although there are certain kinds of websites where having a dynamic page is useful and necessary, you want to avoid creating a dynamic page for any content that you want to have searched and found. A dynamic page, which is individually produced with each new user, presents particular problems for indexing, because they tend to be slightly different at each use.

Prioritize Clarity of Structure

Have you ever been on a website that felt more like a maze than a highway? When you first enter some websites you find yourself on a page whose relationship to the website as a whole is unknown and whose links may not be clear either. The ideal for site creation is to have clarity. You want visitors to be able to easily move through your site and find what they are looking for. You may want to have a website that is like a tunnel. People find what they are looking for and proceed to checkout without being distracted by other aspects of the site. On the other hand, other websites have clearly drawn tabs that allow the visitor to find his or her way around easily, regardless of what page they are on. A lot depends on the particular focus of your site.

Creating a Site Map: If you do not have a site map, you should create one. A site map is web page that lists all the pages of your site in an orderly and systematic way--sort of a table of contents or an index page for your site. Site maps benefit both human visitors and search bots, both of which look to the site map as a way of figuring exactly what is on the site, so you should work to make it clear and logical. You want a human visitor to your site map to be able to survey the sections of your site easily and to be able to see all the pages contained within that section.

There are a number of resources online that can help you create a clear, searchable, XML Sitemap. Google, who initiated and popularized the sitemap concept, recommends XML Sitemaps.com for the creation of sitemaps.

In addition to creating a clear and well-organized sitemap, you should also make sure that you build your site map to auto submit itself to search indexes every time that you add a new page. Auto-submission increases the speed with which your individual pages will start to pop up on SERPs and it also indicates to the index that your page is being actively improved. (Active websites with new pages are one of the criterion used to determine PageRank.) Furthermore, a sitemap allows search bots to have access to pages they might otherwise miss. In many cases, search bots may miss a page that is not easily linked to within your site. If you include this page on the sitemap, however, this increases that chances the search bot will notice it and index it.

Of course, there are some pages on your website that you may not want to be indexed. Why? Let's say that you have two versions of page on your site, one a typical web page in HTML and another a PDF version for those that want to print out that content. Since Google will penalize you for duplicate content, you may want to keep the PDF version from being crawled. In addition to not including the second version in the site map, you will also want to place a line of code in your HTML that indicates to the search bot that you do not want this page indexed.

Focus on Content

A key principle of good website development to remember is that both website users and web crawlers are more favorably disposed to content rather than images and graphics. In fact, search bots will only be able to read the alt tags that you place to describe your images and not the images themselves. Even if your image is of a word or page, the search bot will skip right over it unless that word is included in the alt tag for the image. (An "alt tag" is a line of code you attach to images on your page so that the visually impaired and search bots have some kind of text when they scroll over the otherwise undecipherable image.)

For human visitors to your site, they will also usually prefer to find actual content rather than a series of interesting graphics. (There are, of course, exceptions to this, as when a website is devoted to images of famous paintings or celebrity pics. Although in both of these cases, visitors may be equally interested in the story behind the images to the extent to which they are known.) As you will learn in the next two chapters, how you code this content and how you write it are just as important. For this reason, the vast majority of your page should be made up of words, paragraphs and sentences—not flashy graphics.

Remember the User

Besides all of this, you also want to make your page as user-friendly as well. Remember that your primary target is not really the search engines (though they are a prerequisite to everything else). Your primary target is the human visitor to your website. For this reason, you must focus on making your site as readable and appealing as possible.

Chapter Two: Website Coding

Once you have set up a site whose architecture is attractive to both search engines and visitors, you want to move on to the website coding and the content. Much of SEO coding is completely interconnected to the creation of content for the site, so even as I am discussing the coding, I will be beginning to give you a sense of the next chapter of this book that focuses on the creation of content itself.

When I am referring to the "coding," I am referring to the underlying HTML coding that makes up individual web pages. HTML—Hypertext Markup Language—is the underlying list of instructions that tells your web page everything from what color to use as its background to what images to display and how to display them. It is beyond the scope of this book to tell you all the ins-and-outs of HTML, but in order to successfully execute an SEO campaign you must be able to effectively code your page so it is properly indexed for the SERPs. If you do not create the proper tags, you will have more difficulty getting your page to appear properly on SERPs and this will directly effect your ability to get the kind of quality visitors you are looking for.

Of course, if you do not know HTML, there are platforms you can use that do most of the heavy lifting for you. Wordpress is perhaps the most popular of these. Once you set up your web design, inputting the individual pages is actually fairly straightforward. You should avoid however the kind of service that takes away your ability to alter the underlying HTML. Such services take away a valuable aspect of your ability to SEO properly.

Now is the point at which you will insert those keywords you developed in Part 1. For each page you want to appear on the SERPs, you will want to target one main keyword or keyword phrase. (You might include more than a one keyword phrases, but generally speaking to keep your pages from becoming keyword heavy and difficult to read, you want to have one keyword phrase per page that is your main target while the others are just secondary inclusions.)

This keyword phrase will have to be placed throughout the content of your page, but especially in a few target positions. When it comes to keyword coding you are mainly thinking about making the keyword phrase clear to the search engine indexer so that web users will find your page when they do a search for a particular query. To this end, you have to keep in mind what parts of your page the search bot will pay special attention to and what parts the bot will ignore.

Coding Basics

The central places that you want to be sure to include keywords are in the title, the first line, the meta tags and the subtitles of your web page.

The Main Title Tag: The single most important location to place your central keyword is in the title and title tag for your web page. The title tag is so important because the title is one of the main aspects of the page that is used for indexing. In addition, most websites will use the title of the webpage to create an attachment to the site's main domain name, in order to create a unique URL. For example, if my website URL is http://pizzabook.com and I create a webpage title "5 Tips for Authentic Sicilian Pizza," the Web page URL will usually become http://pizzabook.com/5 tips for authentic sicilian pizza. If the main keyword I am looking to emphasize with this page is "Sicilian pizza," this will work fairly well.

The tag phrase would be written in the HTML coding as follows: "<title>5 Tips for Authentic Sicilian Pizza</title>". The title command indicates that this is the title of the piece and draws search bots to it for indexing. You may notice that the second title tag has a "/" added. This is the punctuation that is added to the second set of commands; the "/" indicates the command ends at this point in the same way that close parenthesis indicate the end of a parenthetical expression.

Meta tags: Meta description tags are explanations of your site contained only within the HTML code (as opposed to the title and header/subtitle tags that usually mirror the title readers actually see within the text itself). Meta tags are another method for indicating to the search engine indexers what the focus of your site is. In addition, meta descriptions will also often appear in SERPs under your site's link by way of explanation. For this reason you want to make your meta description as compelling as possible while keeping it clear and including the appropriate keywords.

To insert the meta description tag, you place a line like the following into the HTML code: <meta name="description" content="Do you want to learn a great recipe for authentic Sicilian pizza? Check out our pizza recipe book here."/> If this were an actual meta description, this might be what appears in the search engines. (Google does not always use meta-descriptions in their SERPs. Google sometimes just picks out an excerpt from your page—often the introduction—instead.)

Take a look at the following search results for a search on "authentic Sicilian pizza."

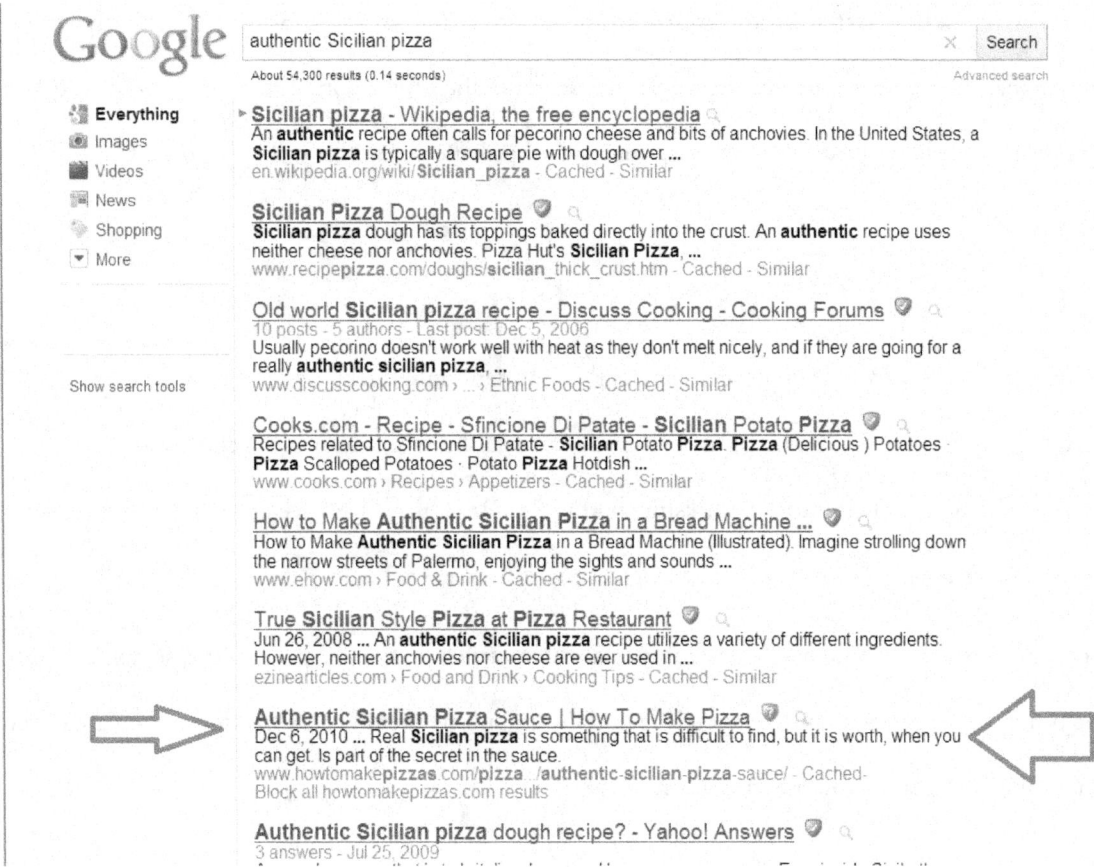

If you look at the entry that I have indicated with my arrows, you find the description, "Real Sicilian pizza is something that is difficult to find, but it is worth, when you can get. Is part of the secret in the sauce." That fairly terribly sentence you can also find both as the introductory sentence of that webpage and inside the meta description code for the page:

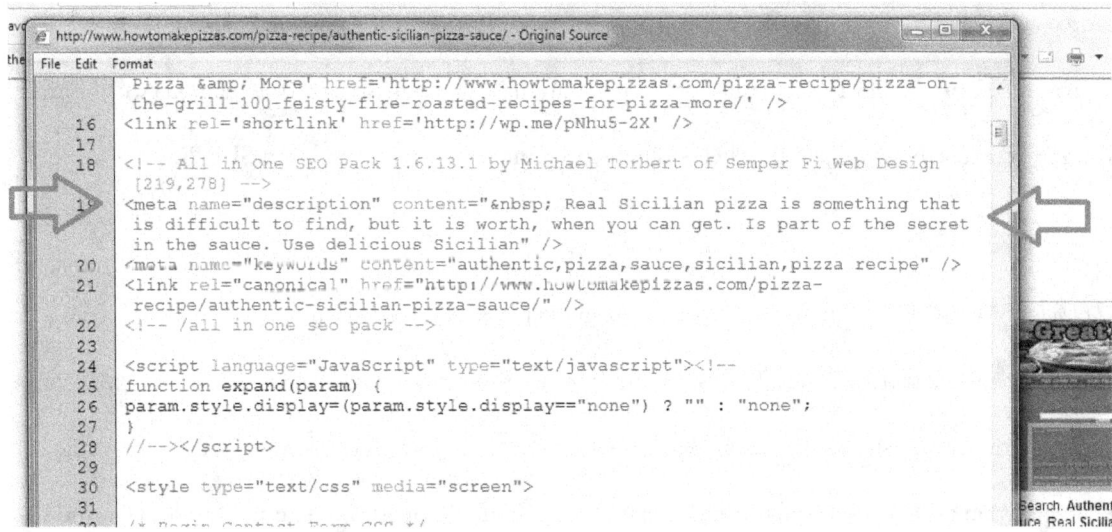

You will notice that it is the same poorly written text emphasizing the keyword "Sicilian pizza." The idea here is to emphasize this descriptive passage by both using it in the source code and as the introductory paragraph of the website. The double emphasis increases the chances that this will be used on the SERP when the site comes up.

There are also *meta keyword tags*. These were once fairly important until the keyword stuffers over-exploited this function. Now however, even though you can still put your keywords into this section, they do little good in terms of helping you improve your listing on the SERPs. On the page we just examined, you can see the meta keyword tag right below the meta tag description line:

<meta name="keywords" content= "authentic, pizza, sauce, sicilian, pizza, recipe"/>. These don't do too much for you in terms of PageRank, but you lose nothing by putting them in. In Wordpress, you are given a prompts and guidelines to inputting this information.

First Line: But how will the search bot know what part of the title is the main keyword? There are actually several ways that the search bot will know this, but one of the ways is that SEO style usually involves repeating the main keyword in the opening lines of the page, usually in the very first sentence. That is one way that you can tell which keywords are being used for SEO by a particular web page without even looking at the source code. So, for example, our webpage might start, "Recipes for traditional Sicilian pizza are passed down in Italian families for generation after generation." The repetition of the main keyword phrase "Sicilian pizza" creates the emphasis that helps build search indexes and by extension SERPs.

Subtitles/Headers: As you are creating your page, you want to pay special attention to how you word your subtitles. Because these subtitles will often correspond to the header tags that you use in your HTML, you want to make sure that the subtitles contain keywords that help search engines discover the central topics of your web page. You need to be careful here, however, because if you overdo it with the header tags and use the same keyword throughout without any variations, you may only succeed in convincing the search indexer that your site is actually keyword spam. For this reason, you should vary your keywords in your headers and subtitles.

A header tag looks like this: <h1>The History of Sicilian Pizza in Italy and America</h1> This is the first subtitle of your article, for example. Notice the "h1". The other subtitles as your page develops will get sequential titles, "h2," "h3," etc. These are also in order of importance and will typically receive varying formats, usually decreasing in size and prominence. Sometimes, your header tags will end up getting your page indexed for a separate search term or a wrinkle related to your search term. So, even though you tried to get your page indexed specifically for those looking for recipes for Sicilian pizza, your first header might end up on a page for "History of Sicilian Pizza" instead.

Other Places Where You Can Use Code to Emphasize Your Keywords

Beyond the basic spots I have mentioned already, there are also other ways that you can use your HTML code to create emphasis for your keywords. One of these places is in the alt description for the images on your page. Since the web crawlers cannot read images, they look to read the alternative descriptions instead. These added description are there so that that the visually impaired will know what is pictured. If you have chosen your images to relate to your text you may find that you can put in a descriptor that also enhances your keyword. For example, if I were to place a photo of an authentic Sicilian pizza on my web page, I might label its alt description as "Photo of an authentic Sicilian pizza." Even if you don't include a keyword, you should put in the alt description because it gives the web crawler more text to read.

There are also a series of other meta tags that help you when it comes to web crawlers. Some of the tags that you put in are interpreted differently by the web crawler than they are by your human readers. The two main examples are *bold/strong* tags and *italics/emphasis* tags:

Bold vs. Strong: When you want to make your words look as if they have been bolded in your HTML, you have the choice between the commands *bold* or *strong,* as in Sicilian pizza. If you write either, the human reader will see **Sicilian pizza**. However, the web crawler will not. The web crawler is programmed only to recognize the *strong* tag as denoting any special form of emphasis and will simply see the *bold* text as of equal value with other words.

Italics vs. Emphasis: The same is true with the *italics* versus *emphasis* distinction. Both look to human readers like italics, but the search engine only recognizes the emphasis tag.

Chap. 7: Content Optimization

Closely tied to website coding is the SEO'd content on your site. Writing compelling content that follows the strictures of SEO is paramount to the success of your SEO campaign and is the most important part of your On-Page SEO efforts. Content should be the focus of your site since it is what draws visitors. Nice graphics and a pleasant clear visual presentation are helpful, but in the end, people come to your site to find a particular answer or product. They are looking for information that will either help them decide to make a purchase or to gather information about a particular topic. So you should have a strong focus on giving them what they came to find.

Google Panda

It is also important to remember that since Google Panda, the focus on well-written, unique content has only grown. Many sites that used to rank well by simply creating slightly altered versions of single texts have suffered sharp drops in ranking during the many quality related updates to Google Panda.

Put simply, Google Panda and its updates are an attempt by Google to improve the quality of search. Google wants its users to find the best most relevant content when they do their searches. For that reason they are constantly tweaking their algorithm to favor what they view as "better content." The Panda updates are large scale upgrades to their algorithm which have made it much more favorable to unique, quality content.

What does this mean for you as a website creator? It means that you should put an even greater emphasis on providing high quality SEO'd content for your site. If ever there was a time to hire better quality writers to create your website content, that time is now.

On the other hand, given how poorly written some of the sites are on the internet, you might be fooled into believing that writing SEO'd content is an easy practice, but, in fact, writing in a compelling fashion while keeping up with the demands of SEO requires more of a writer than many other types of composition. Let us take a look at how SEO works on the level of content:

Keyword Placement

As you may remember from the previous chapter, there are certain locations on your webpage where you should insert your keywords. In the previous section, we mentioned the title, meta tags, headers, and alt tags as some of the places where keywords coded. Except for the meta tags and alt tags, most of these correspond to places in your page content where these keyword phrases should appear as well. Let's consider them individually as we look at the complications that go into creating a well-SEO'd page of content.

Title: As you learned in the previous section, your central keyword phrase should be included in the title of your webpage. So if your main keyword phrase is "Sicilian Pizza," the title of your page should include this keyword phrase. Your title might be, for example, "The Best Sicilian Pizza Recipe," "Sicilian Pizza Recipes from the Old World" or "Make your Own Sicilian Pizza." A good title is short (not more than 40-50 characters) and to the point. "Pizza Recipes from Around the World and Especially Sicilian Pizza" would be both too long and tend to create problems because "Sicilian Pizza" is placed so late in the title that it will probably be ignored by many page indexers. Many web indexers will cut off the ends of titles longer than 40 to 50 characters.

The keyword phrase, of course, needs to be kept exactly as it is. "Sicilian Pizzas" and "Sicilian Vegetarian Pizza" are different keyword phrases. You should also try to get the keyword phrase into the first few words of the post and avoid repeating your keyword more than once in your title.

First Line: Generally, the first line or sentence of the your web site should repeat the main keyword. Often the very first words of an article will be the keyword repeated again. So "Sicilian Pizza..." might be the opening words of your article or should at least be included later in that opening line. Many writers hate this requirement because it limits the possible ways of introducing their topics. Building suspense and a sense of mystery is much more difficult if you have to announce your topic right from the first line. Generally, however, these more literary approaches do not work as well with impatient internet readers as they do in other mediums. Regardless, staying disciplined with this rule is important because it helps emphasize the page's central keyword phrase.

Subtitles: Because your subtitles will generally be linked with header tags, and because search engines give extra weight to these, you should also look to include your primary and secondary keyword phrases in your subtitles. Be careful however not to include the same keyword phrase in every subtitle as this may be interpreted as keyword spam. Ideally, you want to vary the keywords in your subtitles to include more than one keyword phrase and sometimes not to include any keyword at all.

Keyword Density in the Body: In addition to the title, subtitles and opening lines, you will also want to sprinkle your keywords throughout the content section of your webpage. You need to do this carefully however. Search engines are always on the look out for sites attempting to manipulate them into giving up undeservedly higher rankings.

For this reason, web indexers look for a particular target density of keywords. This target seems to be about 3% to 5% of the words on the page. So that means that you should include your keyword 3 to 5 times out of every 100 words. (If your keyword phrase is 2 words long like "Sicilian pizza" you would use it about twice for every hundred words since the larger number of words in your keyword phrase, the larger percentage of keywords they are taking up.) If you do not manage to get up to 3%, then your keyword will not be noticed as significant to the page. If you get more than 5%, you risk having your articles be seen as keyword stuffing.

A Helpful Tip: If you are trying to figure out how many times you have used a particular keyword or keyword phrase, an easy way to do it when you are using Microsoft Word is to use the "Word Count" function under the "Tools" tab to figure out the overall word count and then to use the "Find" function under the "Edit" tab to search how many times a particular word appears. Newer versions of Word will tell you how many instances are found. On older version you use the "Search All" function and it will count them for you.

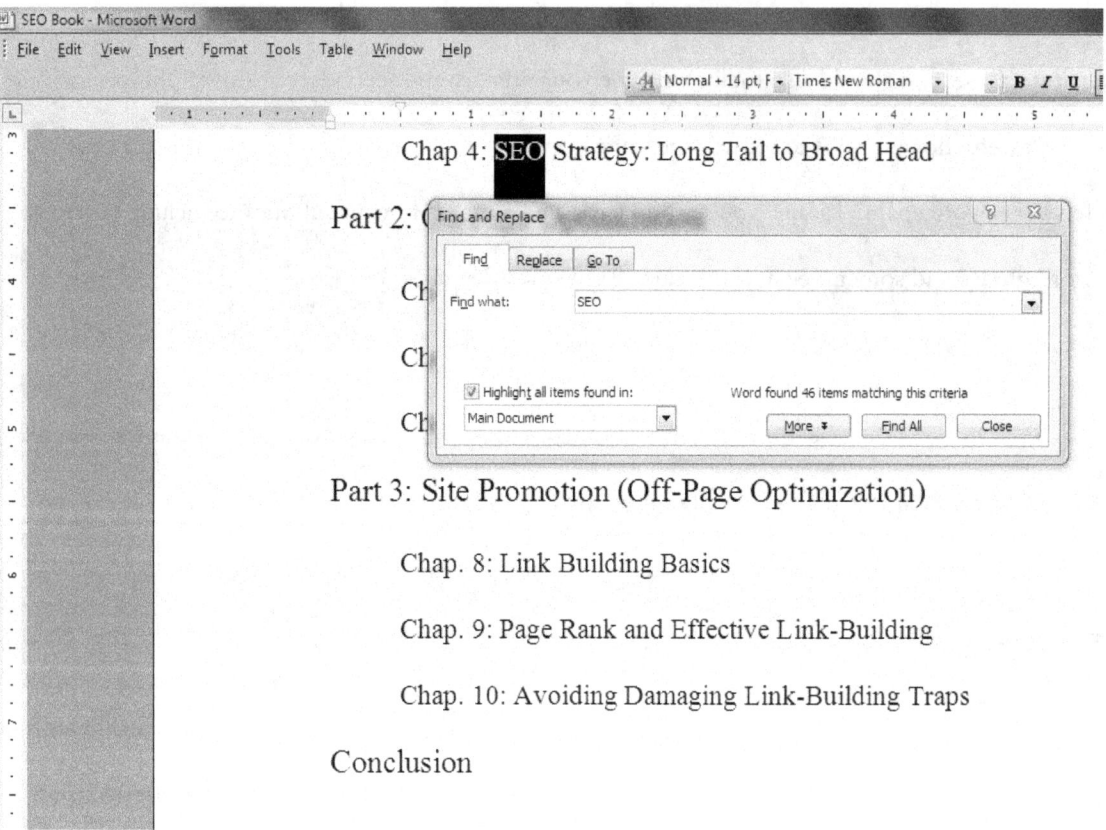

So far, this may not sound too difficult. But consider the following:

Including Keyword Phrases Naturally

One of the problems that comes up for writers trying to inject keywords repeatedly into their texts arises from the manner in which keyword phrases are generated. Google and other search engines generate keywords by monitoring how internet users type out searches into their browsers. So, a phrase like "Sicilian pizza" would be created when Google notices that a certain number of internet users typed this search term. If it didn't already exist, Google would then designate this search term and start to monitor how many users use this phrase for searches. (You can see these stats when you use Google's keyword tool as I described in Part 1.)

However, the problem for web page content writers comes from the way particular web users write their individual searches. When we go to the internet and start to search, we often do not write phrases in proper English. We might for example write "Pizza" first and then, realizing we really want "Sicilian pizza" write "Sicilian" after the word "pizza." If enough users do the same, the search term "pizza Sicilian" is created.

This kind of strange wording creates a real problem for content writers trying to compose content that targets these kinds of phrases. Because although it is a cinch writing a page where the phrase "Sicilian pizza" repeats 3-5% of the time, it is considerably more difficult to fit the phrase "pizza Sicilian" into a page without sounding like English is not your first language.

So how do content writers handle this problem? (Sometimes, of course, website creators just avoid these difficult phrases and stick to the phrases their writers can handle.)

The key is knowing the rules that the search engines follow:

Search Engines Ignore Most Punctuation: One of the most helpful rules to remember about search engines is that they ignore punctuation like dashes, commas and periods. That means that when you are writing the title for your article, you can write "The best kinds of pizza—Sicilian to Brazilian," and the search engine will see: "the best kinds of pizza sicilian to brazilian" thus keeping "pizza sicilian" in the right order. Another favorite of writers is to place difficult phrases like this at sentence breaks. So within the text you might write, "Throughout the world one of the favorite foods is pizza. Sicilian culture was one of the first..." Again, the search engine ignores the period and sees "pizza sicilian" as a unit. The other favorite of writers is the colon: as in, "The best kinds of pizza: Sicilian, vegetarian, and Hawaiian."

Some Exceptions to Ignored Punctuation: There are a few punctuation marks (or more accurately symbols) that are not ignored. Namely: money signs and math symbols like "+" as in "C++". The ampersand, "&" is also not ignored. For most others, however, you can usually use them without having search engines count them as separate keyword phrases.

Other Methods of Emphasizing Keywords

In addition, to the central methods of highlighting keywords that we have mentioned so far, there are also a number of ways that you draw the search engines attention to your keywords that are not as central but that are equally useful.

Include Keywords in Bold and Italics When Possible: Both bolded and italicized text draws the attention of the search engines more than plain text (as long as you use the <strong> and <emphasize> tags as mentioned in the previous chapter), so when possible try to include keywords emphasized in this way in the body of your text.

Introduce Keywords Early: In addition to having keywords in the title and opening lines, you should also look to include keywords in the early sections of your page. Search engines pay less attention to the later portions of your text, so if you have a long document and you wait until the final paragraphs to introduce the bulk of your keyword repetitions, the search engine might not recognize them as the central focus of the page.

Capitalized Words: Search engines view capitalizing much like they view bolding and italicizing, so when possible try to make your keywords into an idea or name that can have the first letters capitalized, as in "I call this recipe, Pizza Sicilian Style."

Other Types of Stylistic Choices Search Engines Love

Search engines generally love a clear logical structure where everything is given its own space and itemized. For this reason, search engines especially like:

Lists and Bullet Points: Lists and bullet points are also an especially good place for keyword phrases because search engines will tend to give individual consideration to each of the bullet points. They are thus equal to other forms of emphasis like italics and bold face. Bullet points and lists are also ideal for web pages because web surfers are far more likely to click and browse through an internet article that has easily digestible information like that presented in lists and bullet points. You have to remember that most internet users feel stressed for time and will rarely give a page more than a few seconds to grab them. If you present the visitor with a thick block of text without visuals or a messy, difficult to comprehend structure, far fewer of them will bother to stick around to find out if what you have to offer them is helpful. Whenever possible, the content of a website should seek to aid the visitor to understand what the site is offering them by the way it structures its content. Lists and bullet points are ideal for this purpose.

Generating Content

One of the criteria used for ranking high on SERPs is the freshness of your content. Especially since Google Panda, this means that in many cases you will need to continue adding to your website. Many sites maintain an active blog for this purpose, or by revising individual pages to introduce new information about their changing business. In many cases, websites need to continue to add individual pages, however. Each new page benefits you, of course, because with each new keyword optimized page, you increase the chances new visitors will reach your site and decide to buy your products or subscribe to your newsletter/s. In many cases larger websites will optimize thousands of pages as an SEO strategy.

The problem, of course, with constantly posting new content to your site is that it requires someone to create that content. Here you have two options: If you are a good writer, you can devote the time to writing the content yourself. If you have an aversion to writing, you can purchase the content. Even though many business owners have the ability to write their own content, they often prefer to purchase it because of the time involved in writing and revising their own copy.

Tips for Purchasing Content:

- *Beware of Plagiarized Content:* If you decide to pay someone to write the content for your website, you will need to be sure to double check that they have not simply lifted the content they create for you from another site. If you use a crowd sourcing website such as *Elance, Odesk,* or *Constant Content,* you should make sure to run the text through a plagiarism detection program before accepting it for your website. This is especially true if you are working with a content provider who does not have much of a history on these websites. A red flag is any mention of previous problems with plagiarism. (On *Constant Content* the site itself monitors for plagiarism and bans writers who abuse this policy.) A good, inexpensive website for checking if the text is original is *Copyscape*. For just a nickel per search you can check entire texts and get detailed lists of site matches for plagiarized content.

- *Do Not Use Duplicate Content:* You want to avoid duplicate content as much as possible, even if it is not technically plagiarized. If the same text appears at more than one location, it is generally a bad idea to repost it. Google, especially since Panda, looks unfavorably at repeated content as far as SERP position goes.

- *Strive For Quality Writing:* Although much of the writing you find on the internet is amateurish or grammatically suspect at best, you should always strive to have quality writing on your website. (Even if that quality write is in an informal conversational style of the kind that is common on blogs.) Many visitors will judge the professionalism of a website by the quality of the writing on it. If much of your content is filled with grammatical problems or other careless errors, visitors may start to suspect that the services you offer will be similarly shoddy. If you hire a "writer," make sure they can actually write. This seems obvious, but you would be surprised how often those claiming to be *writers* can barely put two grammatically correct sentences together. (In addition, be careful when hiring SEO writing companies, as they will often subcontract your project to less skilled writers once they have won the bid.)

- *Avoid Fluff:* Similar to the previous point, your website should also offer useful, preferably actionable information. Many of the writers you find on the internet are experts of the "churn-n-burn" style of SEO writing: lot's of useless information created in a style that attracts search engines but that leaves readers cold because it lacks substance. This kind of airy writing might give your site an initial bump on the SERPs but will tend to fade quickly as visitors, disappointed with the lack of substance on your site beat a hasty retreat back to the results page. You may have to pay writers a bit more for tracking down actionable information, but the results are well worth it in the long term.

Content creation becomes even more of an issue in Off-Page SEO, when creating fresh work that is similar to but not identical with your website's content is one of the keys to driving traffic. In the next section, we will discuss even more strategies for creating content.

Part 3: Off-Page Optimization

Chapter 8: Understanding the Importance of Link Building

Of all the parts of SEO, Off-Page Optimization requires the most patience and is the most labor intensive because it involves creating content on multiple other sites. If you have done the first two parts of SEO (chosen a powerful set of keywords and optimized your pages so that search engines can read them), then you can now begin the difficult task of promoting your site and getting it noticed by search engines and other sites. This part of SEO is often referred to as "Link Building." The idea is fairly simple: you want to get as many valid sites to link back to your site as possible. (In SEO, these incoming links are referred to as "Backlinks.") Simple though the idea may be, actually getting these links can get quite complicated, as you will see.

Why are backlinks important?

Backlinks are one of the central criteria Google uses in order to determine your PageRank. Google's reasoning for putting so much faith in backlinks is that if a lot of different websites related to your topic link to yours, then your popularity must be justified; other sites in the know must be linking to yours because you are offering them useful and compelling information.

Sometimes this kind of linking actually does happen naturally. Websites like Wikipedia, for example, get a large number of links from sites that simply find their information useful. Everyone from business people to college professors will link to Wikipedia pages (even if, Wikipedia is favorite target of criticism for PhD's at universities). Regardless of their reasons for linking, these websites help build a site's reputation and PageRank.

However, most websites are not able to create these kinds of links passively. In a crowded internet landscape, standing out and getting noticed do not happen without a fair bit of self-promotion. So, in order to carry out this part of SEO, sites must initially create the outwardly appearance of being a popular site by convincing other sites to link to them. (In many cases, sites will simply never be linked to "passively" and have to earn every link they receive. If a site sells sprockets, for example, it is unlikely they will find niche sprocket communities that really love their site and want to link to it of their own accord.) Many sites, as they begin to get some traction will find that some of their pages containing useful and compelling information will get linked to without it being a primary part of the site's link building campaign but these unsolicited occurrences are often few and far between. In large part, you will have to work to get your links.

There are other reasons, other than increasing you PageRank, that make link building important—perhaps not the least of which is that Google and other search engines find and index sites through web links. If you start getting a lot of links, the chances are good that the Google Bot will follow one of the links and find your site. (As you will see, however, you can also help this along by submitting your site to Google, the other search engines and search directories.)

The Power of Linking

Before we move on to outlining the strategies for getting these all important links, we need to get a sense of the power of individual links and how this power works. Here are some points you must understand about links before we continue:

- *First, not all links are created equal:* That is, some links are worth more than others—it is not just about getting the largest number of links, although numbers do definitely matter. Links, however, from high ranking pages are worth more than links from pages that hardly register at all. So, if your Aunt Betty links to you from her cat's blog, this will not be weighed the same as if The New York Times web page links to you. In addition, most SEO experts believe the Google algorithm values links coming from *.edu* and *.gov* sites more than other sites. Expert sites and directories also are valued higher than regular sites. So finding quality links should be a major part of your strategy.

- *Reciprocal Links Virtually Nullify Each Other:* If you agree to link to someone else's page and they agree to link to yours, this tends to just cancel itself out with neither one of you gaining much from the experience. This is especially true if pretty much all your links are of the reciprocal variety. The key is to get *one way, inbound links from other website whenever possible.*

- *Purchased Links Not Only Don't Help Your Rank, They Actually May Hurt It:* There are a number of sites on the internet known as "link farms," where you can purchase links to your webpages. Unfortunately for those who do so, search engines know about these sites as well, and they will not only not give you credit for these links, they will actually penalize you for them.

- *Beware of No-Follow Links:* Many websites also lure you in with superior PageRank and get you to buy links or promise to exchange links, but then, the links turn out to have a "no follow" tag written into the anchor text (the code that points the hyperlink to your web page). It will often look like this, for example: *<a href="http://www.myexample.com/" rel="nofollow">My Example</a>* The *rel="no-follow"* section of the tag tells the search engines not to pay attention to the link. Thus, you may get some more visitors but the search engines will not give you credit for being linked to by the "no-follow" page.

- *Sites with Similar Themes are Given More Weight:* Links from sites that have similar themes to yours are given more weight than those that do not have similar themes. This matching of site themes is a necessarily imprecise art for the search engines, but they can generally tell when something is rather fishy. This is how JC Penny got into trouble recently when they were using a link building strategy that involved placing links to their site on physics forums and other similarly unrelated sites. So, taking our pizza recipe book example up again, your page would get more credit for getting a link from a website that deals with recipes and cooking than it would from physics sites. (Even if it was a professor giving his students a tasty recipe as reward for completing an on-line physics lab.)

- *Link Maturity:* Believe it or not, search engines also prefer links that have been well-established, so you should not expect to experience the full effect of a link from a very popular site right away.

One more aspect of links that you should not forget is that they also help categorize your site for search engines. That is why—as you will find out a bit later—it is important for the links to your site to be tagged with keywords from your list.

Outgoing Links

You might wonder however, whether it is bad to have outgoing links. Since reciprocal links tend to cancel each other out in terms of improving PageRank, is it then the case that every time that you have an outgoing link, you are actually giving away your power? Will your page and website lose some of its ranking because you linked from your pizza recipe site to an Italian recipe site?

The answer is actually complicated. SEO insiders generally believe that when you link from your page to another, your page does not lose any PageRank. In other words, you still have the same number of links coming into your page and you will still get roughly the same placement on SERPs for the keyword phrases you have optimized.

However, when you link to a page that is outside your site, the other pages on your site may lose some of their PageRank, which indirectly means that the linking page loses PageRank as well. Why is this the case? The reason is this. If we consider the *ranking* power of each individual page to be like a series of shares, then each time that you link out of the page, it is like giving a portion of those shares away. If you have four links on a page with one of them going to another page on your website while the other three go to pages on other websites, then you have just given away ¾ of your page's ranking power to other sites rather than keeping it within your site. In this way, outbound links from your site reduce its overall PageRank.

Of course, you may have more difficulty getting others to link to your site if your site is hermetically sealed within itself and only links within its own pages. We will answer this problem in the next the chapter.

In addition, the more links there are on an outside page linking to your page, the less help that backlink will give you, because the more its power will be divided up between your site and all the others that the page links to. So, if the page linking to your page has 100 links on it, you only get 1% of its boost to your PageRank.

Careful with Broken Links: You should also take care with your own, outbound links. You need to make sure that your outgoing links do not deliver your site visitors to a "404 Error" page, because these broken links will not only disappoint your visitors but will make the Google Bot think that you are a decrepit site that may have been abandoned by its owners.

To make sure that your links continue to be valid, download a program like Link Checker. Link Checker will automatically inform you as you site links go bad so that you can refresh and relink before your site is negatively affected.

Chapter 9: Link Building 101

So how do you go about creating backlinks to your site so that you can increase your PageRank, do better on the SERP's, and ultimately get those conversions that are the reason from going through all this trouble?

It is all about SITE PROMOTION!

The first thing that you have to keep in mind as you are pursuing links is that the entire goal of this aspect of SEO is to promote your site. You want to get people to notice your site and ideally, to link to your site, so that visitors, especially visitors who actually have an interest in what your site is about, will click for a visit. To that end, you should keep in mind that getting links is a means to an end. They are valuable for increasing PageRank and your presence on SERPs but they are also valuable in and of themselves because each one provides web surfers yet another possible entryway into your site.

For this reason, you should cast your net far and wide, and find more than one way of getting links to your site.

Submitting Your Site to the Search Engines and Directories

Eventually as you build backlinks to your site, web crawlers, spiders and search bots will discover one of these links, follow it back to your website, and then index it. During the period beforehand, however, while you are invisible and waiting, it can be quite frustrating to not even register anywhere on the SERP's.

One thing that you can do to try to speed up the process is to submit your site or an XML Sitemap of your site to the search engines. Here is where you can go to submit your website to do this:

For Google it is www.google.com/addurl.html

For Yahoo it is http://search.yahoo.com/info/submit.html

And for MSN/Live Search it is http://search.msn.com/docs/submit.aspx

Just as useful is to submit an XML Sitemap to the Big Three. An XML Sitemap is a coded version of the kind of sitemap that you might create for your site, except that unlike that sitemap it is not really for human visitors to read. An XML Sitemap is created specifically for the bots that visit your site so that they can more easily map all of the pages. (In fact, it is in many cases invisible to human visitors.) By submitting it to the search engines directly, you increase (but do not ensure) that your website will get indexed.

Indexing is not automatic however, nor does submitting ensure that all your pages will get indexed and that you will start appearing on search results. But since it does increase the chances of the process being expedited it is certainly worth doing. Anything that you can do to speed things up a bit in the beginning will give you a greater sense of forward momentum.

You can also register your site with a number of minor search engines that focus on much narrower audiences. They are small so they get a lot less traffic than the Big Three, but they tend to have fairly committed niche audiences. A good way to get registered for these smaller search engines is to purchase an *automated search engine submission service/program*. If you do a search on "search engine submission" you will find a number of these services. You can also find programs that will do the trick such as *Submit Wolf* and *Dynamic Submission*. (Both are fee-based programs not free, in case you wondering.)

Submitting to Directories

In addition to submitting to search engines, you can also submit your website to search directories. Search directories are basically what the World Wide Web was before Google's algorithm changed the entire landscape of the Information Highway. In the mid to late 90's, Yahoo's directory was the main way that people found information on the web. This was a human based (rather than program based) method of organizing websites into categories rather than search pages.

Here is what the Open Directory (one of the largest directories) looks like:

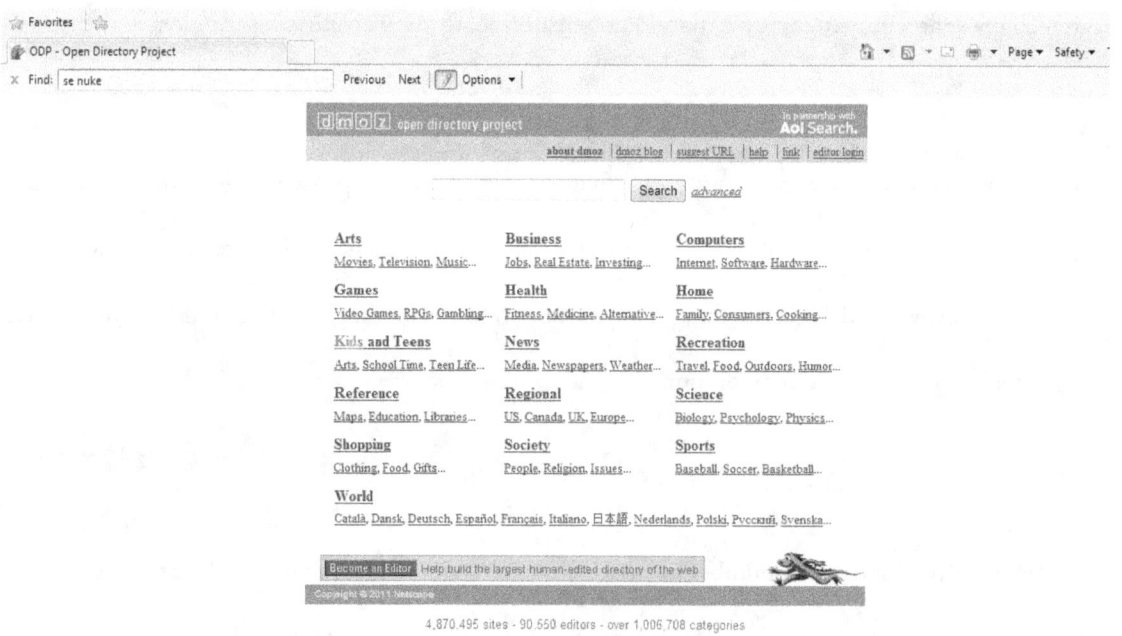

Directories are still organized in this manner and though Google and the search engine model has pretty much won the day in terms of web users, there are still a smaller but significant number of people who prefer to find their information via the directory format.

In addition to providing extra traffic to your sites, directories also offer a number of other benefits. Directories are regularly crawled by search engines looking for new places on the internet to index, which means they provide yet another way search engines might come across your site. Directory listings also count as one way links to your site, which will help with PageRank. Finally, you can usually create a keyword-specific link to your site which, along with the directory's categorization of your site, helps Search Indexes to categorize your site.

There are, of course, some major differences between search engines and web directories. Beyond the fact that directories are organized manually by humans and the fact that directories are categorized, another major difference between directories and search engines is that most directories limit the number of places that your website can appear within the directory. This means that every time that you submit to a directory you must examine it to determine which category works best for your website.

Finally, be aware that most directories require you to submit information about your site, and then in many cases they will take some time reviewing your site to make sure that it deserves to be on their directory. This can take a matter of weeks but is well worth it for the larger directories: Yahoo! Directory (located within the Yahoo search site though no longer prominently on the home page as it once was), Google Directory, and GoGuides.Org.

Some directories also try to charge you for the "privilege" of being included in their categories. This form of paid inclusion program is rarely worth it, especially when the directory is not one of the Big Three. Even then, you can probably avoid paying for it.

Asking for Backlinks

The bread and butter of link building is still just asking for them from other sites. You might begin by hitting up your family and close friends to link to your site from theirs—if they have any--, but quickly you will want to turn to asking those which have sites on the same subject as yours. How should you go about finding these related sites? You can't after all, ask your competitors to give you a plug on their sites. Here are few ideas:

- *Keyword Search:* One effective way to find sites like yours is to use the keyword phrases you have chosen—and maybe even some of those that you decided not to use—to find other sites that are like yours.
- *Do Internet Searches for Sites Similar to Yours:* If you are in a particular field, it is helpful to do searches for businesses like your own. For example, our pizza recipe book might be able to find sites that specialize in recipes and books.
- *Look at the Links of Related Sites:* Similar sites often link to each other as you are attempting to do. When you find one site, research their outgoing links to discover other sites with similar themes.

Composing Effective Backlinks

Before we move on to other methods of getting backlinks to your site, we need to get a better sense of how you want to have your links composed. (In many cases, of course, you will have little say in how your link is composed by the owners of other sites—after all you are asking them to do you a favor. But you can try to sway their decisions by gently suggesting ways they might tag their links to your site. And, in those areas where you do have control, you should pay close attention to how you create your backlinks.)

You should also keep in mind a few things about the sites that link to your site:

Avoid Banned Sites: Be careful that the site that you are creating links to or from is not a banned site by Google. Sites may be banned for a number of reasons. Some sites that you should not get links from are fairly obvious like adult sites and gambling sites, and we have already mentioned link farms. Some are less obvious on the face of it however. For example, sites can be banned for hiding links or for "cloaking"—creating a web page whose content doesn't match with its underlying text code in an attempt to fool web crawlers and other site indexers. If you get links from or send links to them, not only will they not count towards but they may actually hurt your PageRank.

So how do you know if the site you are considering has been banned? Several sites on the internet contain simple ban detection tools that allow you to input the site domain and find out whether or not it is banned.

Link Website PageRank: In addition to making sure they are sites in good standing you should also seek to get websites with better page rank to link to your site. The weaker the linking site, the less useful the link. So a link from a PageRank 1 or 2 site does very little to help your own PageRank, while a PageRank 8 website link is worth spending a fair amount of effort trying to get. PageRank 4 and 5 and higher are the usual measures websites use as a cut-off point for looking for linking.

BE CAREFUL HOWEVER: You should avoid making your links seem unnatural. You don't want all the links to be from PageRank 5 and 6 sites for example. You should try to mix in some lower ranking sites as well, so that your linking does not look simply like link building.

How do you figure out the PageRank for the site that is linking to you? Generally, the best way to do this is to look at the home page for the site. Use the Google Toolbar PageRank bar to determine the website's PageRank (as I mentioned back in Part 1 when discussing PageRank).

Why not use the linking page's PageRank? The linking page presents two problems in terms of PageRank. First, the linking page may not give you a complete picture of its own PageRank. Google does not reliably measure the secondary pages of websites. More importantly however, the linking page's PageRank is likely to be less stable since an individual web page may been created only recently or may not have been completely indexed. Of course, if an individual page does register with a high PageRank, that is a good sign.

Similarly Themed Sites: As mentioned earlier you should strive to find sites with themes similar to yours from which to get backlinks. This is fairly clear. Even if, however, the overall site is not related to yours, it may be enough to have the page have a connection to your theme. So, for example, if our Pizza Recipe site gets a link from a website that focuses on Italian history, it would work best if the link appeared on a page about Italian cuisine or linked to our "authentic Sicilian recipe" page from the website's page about Sicilian history. (The link should also ideally point out this connection.)

Composing Anchor Text

Put simply, anchor text is the title of your back link including both the underlying link code and the content portion that appears for human readers. When you have control of placing your links in yourself and can submit pages with HTML tagging attached you should keep your SEO strategy in mind. The best way to illustrate how to do this is by showing you an example. Let us say we are creating a link back to my business website www.websitedesignbyadam.com, but I want to emphasize the keyword phrase "affordable Los Angeles website design". This is how I would code the backlink: <a href="http://www.websitedesignbyadam.com/">Affordable Los Angeles Website Design</a>. A visitor reading the page would come upon a hyperlink labeled Affordable Los Angeles Website Design.

You do not want to forget about keyword density however. As you might remember, you do not want to overuse keywords in your content. This is just as true when it comes to your backlinks. If the search engine indexer notices that all of the links to a particular webpage have the exact same keywords, it will read this as keyword spam as well. Ideally, you will have a mix of keyworded backlinks feeding into your site. To the extent that this is under your control, you should look to vary them and make them seem relatively natural. For example, for our Pizza Recipe site's Authentic Sicilian Pizza Recipe page we might have a link from a history site that reads "Historically Authentic Sicilian Pizza Recipe" whereas from a parenting webpage we might have "Quick and Easy Recipe for Sicilian Pizza." Remember that even the slightest of differences in word order create different keyword phrases.

Suggesting Anchor Text for Other Sites: Of course you do not always have control over what other site administrators and authors use as their anchor text and it can seem a little heavy handed to demand they structure links on their sites according to your specifications. If, however, you ask them courteously and make it easy for them to copy and paste your anchor text from your request e-mail, you may find webmasters are more likely to place your links as you would like.

If you notice any problems with the link that has been created with your link text, such as a misspelling or inaccuracies (such as claiming the linked to page is about one thing when it is about another), then it is best to contact the website as early as possible since the author is most likely to alter the link soon after he or she has created the page than months late when they may not even remember who you are or what they wrote.

Tip for Getting Links: One thing that you can do to help other web creators to link to your site in the manner you would like is to create a "Terms of Use" page in which you outline how you would like your site linked to and give readers an anchor text sample they can easily copy and paste into their webpages.

Other Places from Which to Get Links

I have already mentioned search directories, acquaintances, and related websites as places where you should seek backlinks. A number of other sources can also be useful for this purpose. Here are a few:

- *Business Groups and Associations:* If you are a member of a particular business group or career association, contact them to find out if you can have a link to your business placed on their sites. In many cases this is now fairly common. For example, veterinarians in a local area will often register with the local vet association and have their names and businesses listed at the association website, along with a brief description of their professional interests. Often you are allowed to write this description and to place a link in the description. Do not miss this opportunity.
- *Business Partners:* Do not forget to ask the companies you partner with and purchase from to include a link to your website. Most businesses have partnering businesses that they use all the time. These are often the perfect venues for links. In addition, businesses who you do business with are far more likely to feel compelled to give you a plug because of your working relationship.

Find Sites that Are Linking to Sites Similar to Yours: One of the best ways to find sites to link to yours is by tracking down sites that already link to other sites like yours—sometimes even to your competitor's sites. Do not assume just because a site links to your competitor's website that they do not want to link to yours. Often, in fact, sites would love to give their readers more than one option when it comes to linking but just are not sure which site they should choose. Finding and contacting these sites can be quite fruitful for both PageRank and for traffic in general.

But how do you find these linking websites. After all, even though figuring outbound links is easy (you just look at the hyperlinks on the pages), finding the inbound links is not. You can find some of the inbound links through Google and Yahoo. Both Google and Yahoo! offer ways to find out the number of links to a site and some of the domain names, but to get a more complete list of backlinks into a site you will probably need to use one of the link popularity programs or websites. There are some very basic link popularity programs on the web, which will list the pages connecting to a website. The paid programs can give you a fuller, more detailed picture however that usually includes everything from the PageRank of the linking page to counts of the total number of links on the linking pages and estimates of the approximate value of the links.

None of these tools are perfect, but they will give you a more than adequate list with which to find websites that will make good hosts for your links.

Writing Intensive Ways of Creating Backlinks

One of the main difficulties you will encounter when it comes to creating backlinks is being able to offer the owner of the linking website something in return for hosting a link to your page. Since linking to another page can be seen as a form of losing PageRank, most website owners will be reluctant to do so without a good reason. Of course, you will find some websites that would like to link to yours because they like your site and think their readers will find value in knowing about it, but this is only a small segment of those website owners who you will contact.

Most websites will want something in return for linking to your site. The most common request is for a reciprocal link—you link to them and they link to you. As you know by now, however, reciprocal links do not help you much and if you have too many such links they can actually hurt you. You can also try to do a more complicated three way trade with a third site so that all the links to each of your sites look like strictly inbound links, but this is both time consuming and limited in its feasibility.

Ultimately you must have something to offer sites to make it worth their while to host your link. More often than not, content is what you can produce that websites want. As you might recall, one of the criterion Google uses to determine PageRank is how much fresh content a site produces. Many sites depend on tons and tons of fresh content. But getting original, valuable content is not that easy.

This is where you can come in. Creating content for another site in exchange for a link back to yours is a win-win. It offers the other site the content they want for cheap (or occasionally you can even get a tiny bit of a kickback on some content sites), and it gives you what you want, the backlink. In addition, however, you will also be able to interest readers from the linking website in the content that you have to offer on your site. So even though they haven't even linked to your site yet, you are already beginning to win them over with your valuable information and, hopefully, wit.

Creating your own content for linking websites also offers you the benefit of far greater control over your message. Although it is possible that the website owner will alter your content for his or her own uses, generally, most linking websites will present the content you post to their sites in the way the you want to have it presented.

There are several different venues on which you can post content and get a backlink in return:

- *Guest Blogging:* the most traditional venue for a content for backlink trade is via a guest blog. In a guest blog, you write an article for posting on someone else's website and they give you both author credits and present your backlink so their readers can check out more of your content. You might, for example, write a post or article about the history of Sicilian Pizza for an Italian history and culture website and leave a link to your Sicilian Pizza Recipe page at the end of the article.
- *Posting Comments to Related Discussion Forums:* Another really effective way to get backlinks and especially to increase traffic, is to stay active with discussion forums related to your website topic or theme. Although some websites will not allow you to leave backlinks and will police forums to make sure commenters comply, many will and if you leave relevant, compelling replies to forum topics you are likely to attract exactly the kind of conversion ready site visitors that you would love to have. In addition, many of these forums are listed on SERPs when web surfers type in the same question as the forum title. So, for example, when a web surfer types in

the search question: "What is it like living in Santa Monica California?" they may find your forum post describing rent prices or crime data, and link back to your Santa Monica article on your real estate site.

- *Newsletters:* Both physical newsletters and web newsletters can help you increase your web traffic and often get backlinks in a much more natural fashion. Newsletters put out by industry groups or communities are a fairly effective way of reaching an audience who is more likely to pay attention to your message. Web newsletters which are often sent by e-mail are usually also posted on line, either at the website for the initiating community/group or when search engines later index the letter. Physical newsletter for local newspapers and smaller geographical associations often also find their way onto the web and more and more local groups are migrating onto the web as both a cost saving measure and purely for the convenience of it. Even if they don't lead directly to web links, however, they do provide yet another possible driver for your web traffic.

- *Creating your Own Newsletters and Web Announcements:* Another useful way to indirectly get web links is to e-mail regular announcements about what your business or website is up to. For example, if you have a nightclub with a website, you might attach a request for visitors who sign up for your newsletter to add a link to your site on their own websites and blogs.

Producing Content

As you have no doubt gathered by now, creating all of this content both on your site and on linking sites can be quite a chore. If you are a pretty good writer, you may be able to handle writing all the content for your own site, but do you really have the time to produce all of this off-site content as well? Do you have time to do that and still actually run your business and have a life?

Let us consider the options:

Creating Original Content: One option is writing your own content. Unless your site is very small and you intend to keep it fairly small, then this is probably a job for more than one person. If you have a company with several strong writers, then you may be able to produce your work in house. Otherwise you will probably need to hire a small team of writers.

Duplicate Content: You could also send out several versions of the same article each with its own link back. There are a couple of problems with this. First and foremost, Google does not like duplicate content and will often penalize the sites that use it by only displaying one of the pages in question. This is a problem for you because that means that the linking pages will receive less traffic. In addition, many web masters simply do not want duplicate content.

Some SEO specialists believe that you can change only the opening paragraph of your article and leave the rest the same and that that will count as a "unique" article as far as the search engines are concerned. I have not found this to be case. The articles have to be far more varied than this or they will be marked as duplicates.

Automated Content: You can also find a number of different web programs that can help you generate "unique" content—or at least content that will seem unique. This kind of automated content is known as *spinning*. Here are the basics of how it works: You start by writing one unique article on one of your website topics. Then you take that first version of your article and with the help of the spinning program, you begin to make variations on it. Typically a program will have you come up with two to three synonyms for words in each sentence and then come up with at least one alternate version of each sentence. This is actually fairly difficult and time consuming work because the synonyms you find must work just about as well in each of the sentences you create-as must the alternate sentences.

Here is an example of how a spun sentence might look: "This is [actually/truly/really] fairly [difficult/hard/complicated] and time-consuming work, because the synonyms you [find/discover/choose] must work [just about/almost/nearly] as well in each of the [sentences/phrases/contexts] you create as they must in the [alternative/secondary/replacement] sentences." When you place this sentence into the spinning machine it will give you a slightly different iteration each time. For example, it might come out "This is actually fairly complicated and time-consuming work, because the synonyms you find must work almost as well in each of the phrases you create as they must in the secondary sentences."

Or : This is actually fairly complicated and time-consuming work, because the synonyms you discover must work just about as well in each of the phrases you create as they must in the replacement sentences."

Now, although these turned out fairly well, in many cases the writers have difficulty finding alternate sentences and words that work just as well since so much of writing has to do with finding the exact word. When you have this number of alternates, language can become a bit awkward and clunky in spots.

Nevertheless, spinning software is sometimes the only way for content generators to get their work out to high number of hosting sites and to boost PageRank inexpensively. Many SEO submission software programs, like SEO Nuke, a relatively new submission program, will include spinning software as well as automated linking software.

Deciding which type of approach to use will have a lot to do with your overall SEO strategy.

Conclusion

For my final comments about SEO I want to look at the territories into which Search Engine Marketing reaches. In addition to doing traditional SEO, you may want to extend your campaign to include PPC and SMO. These two extensions of SEO may not be right for every campaign, but increasingly both are being used in conjunction with classic SEO strategies to maximize the reach of your marketing efforts.

Pay Per Click Advertising

Let's begin by looking at what is often called SEO's *evil brother*, Pay Per Click. Pay Per Click—abbreviated PPC—is a method by which you rent a keyword (what Google calls an "Adword") so that when a user searches the term, an ad for your website pops up above the organic results—typically marked off in the top three slots. When someone clicks on the ad, the ad placer gets billed for that click—a "click charge." The idea is for the business to get placed on that all important first SERP, right at the top and to get the kind of traffic from it that is ready to convert.

When done well, PPC can really help a business boost revenues. Pay Per Click makes it so that you do not technically have to optimize your site page for that term and you will still get a lot of traffic from it—if it is done correctly.

However, to create a successful Pay Per Click campaign, you will have to do more than just buy up a lot of Ad Words and wait. In other words, I want to emphasize that you should not think of Pay Per Click as being opposed to SEO. In fact, conducting a successful Pay Per Click campaign requires you to set virtually the same initial groundwork as you would for an SEO campaign. By which I mean that you will still have to research keywords and figure out which ones will drive the right kind of traffic to your site. Otherwise, you may get increased page views but not increased conversions. Long tail keywords are often still the most effective way to get this traffic, since these long tail Adwords are likely to be the most cost effective.

In fact, a PPC campaign is best conducted in conjunction with an SEO campaign, each complimenting and strengthening the other.

What does a Pay Per Click campaign cost?

The price varies greatly, ranging from as little as a penny per click to as much as $20 to $25 dollars. (There are rumors of some very high value keywords going for as much $50/click, but these higher rangers are extremely rare.) A lot depends on the *competition* for the keyword and the *click through rate*. The competition of a keyword is the amount of demand that exists for a particular keyword. It works somewhat like a bidding system. The more customers want to buy a keyword, the higher the cost goes.

Google, however, puts some added criteria onto the ads it hosts on its SERPs. Namely it looks for two things:

1. Will Google users find the ad *relevant*?

2. Will Google profit from the ad?

These two criteria are, of course, interrelated. The more satisfied users are with their searches the more likely they are to favor Google over its competitors, like Yahoo and Bing.

Part of the way Google determines if your ad is relevant is by analyzing its *click-through rate*. The click-through rate is the percentage of times users clicked your ad relative to the number of page views. If your click through rate is very low, then Google will judge that your ad is not addressing its users' needs and charge you more for continuing your campaign. For example, let us say that my ad gets 100 clicks while yours gets 50 on most days. If Google is charging me $3 dollars per click, they may charge you $7.50 per click to rank above me (250% of my cost), since your ad is only half as effective as mine. That quickly adds up: $300/100 clicks for me vs. $750/100 clicks for you.

For this reason, of course, it is important to create ads that work. Otherwise you will get the worst of both worlds fewer clicks and higher costs.

Determining whether a price for a particular Adword is worth it requires you to do a cost benefit analysis. If the percentage of customers converting from clicking on your ad is high enough to justify the expense of getting them to click, then you can justify your PPC campaign. So an upper end jewelry store might be able to justify $15/click if one of ten clickers buys $300+ in jewelry perhaps. On the other hand, if you sell $5 hand crafted thimbles that rarely net you more than $20 from any one customer, it's probably not worth it if each click is going to cost you any more than $1 (even that would probably be too high).

The point with all this, is that a PPC campaign requires just as much thought and analysis as your SEO campaign. You will have to spend almost as much time creating effectively crafted ads and monitoring to make sure that individual keywords are justifying their costs. Perfecting your landing page, excluding negative keywords (like "free") and honing your *call to action* will replace the issues related to SEO, though not completely.

Social Media Optimization

Another way to promote your website is through Social Media Optimization (also referred to as SMO, for short). In most cases social media is not really a part of link building because most types of social media do not help your PageRank directly. (Twitter for examples automatically pastes "No Follow" code into you tweets so that you will send only human viewers via your links—no link juice.) However, if you have the time and resources to devote to this kind of marketing it can help drive traffic to you site, and generally this will translate into higher conversions and often more link juice when some of those visitors link to you site from their own.

Social Media Optimization is the hot topic of site promotion these days, and most forward thinking marketers believe that there is a great deal of value still available to be tapped in the social media landscape. At the time of this writing this is a rapidly changing landscape as well, with a fluidity that makes it difficult to fully explain in a short space. For certain kinds of businesses, however, these other forms of social media are crucial to effectively creating a web presence. It's beyond the scope of this current book to take an in-depth look at all of the kinds of social media and how they relate to SEO (that could really be a book onto itself), but let's take a look at a few of the major forms of social media individually so that you get a sense of the lay of the land:

Facebook: Of course, the three-hundred pound gorilla in social networking these days is Facebook. Having a Facebook page is quickly becoming like having a phone number or an e-mail address. People, especially those Mark Zuckerberg's age and younger, take having a Facebook page for granted and businesses are also now a strong presence on Facebook.

How does this relate to SEO?

In a narrow sense it does not. Up until recently, search engines only partly indexed Facebook pages, usually stopping at the public profile page that nonmembers have access to. It was not clear that having a Facebook page created much more of a web presence in terms of link building. However, recently Facebook has started to make their site more search engine friendly by allowing users to do things like create an individualized page name (as opposed to just using the user's actual name) and having spaces that you can keyword like you would any other webpage. These changes have increased the opportunities for SEO and started to narrow the gap between Facebook and Google.

You need to be careful, however, since there is a bit of an anti-marketing ethos on Facebook, and any kind of page that strikes other Facebook users as too "spammy" may find itself very lonely. So when including keywords in your About Page or other tabs, for example, you need to do it with much more subtlety than you do on a regular website.

In addition, you should also be aware that many marketers consider Facebook a bad place for finding clients for the businesses they are marketing. Instead, they largely consider Facebook a good place to help build your business or career brand. Brand building of this kind can be time-consuming work and you should have a clear reason for including Facebook as part of your marketing strategy.

Google Plus: Google, of course, is now trying to compete on the same playing field as Facebook. Google Plus, is Google's version and it is sure to even better integrated with search engines than Facebook. For this reason you should use Google Plus much as you would Facebook.

LinkedIn: Another social networking site worth mentioning is the up-and-coming LinkedIn. LinkedIn is basically Facebook for the career oriented. Unlike Facebook where it is not uncommon to see photos from college frat parties, LinkedIn is more about presenting a professional front and networking with other professionals in your industry or a related one.

In terms of SEO, LinkedIn is much like Facebook. It is more about establishing a presence than getting back links. (We could put MySpace in the same category as well.)

Microblogging with Twitter: One avenue of non-traditional blogging that you can use to help build site traffic is Twitter. Given the amount of attention it has gotten recently, I hardly need to tell you that Twitter is part social network, part blogging platform, and part public e-mailing platform.

You should treat Twitter roughly as you would any other blog. Since search engines crawl Twitter, it is possible to keyword your tweets for SEO. Despite this, however, you should not over do it. The main goal of Twitter should still be to build traffic and brand building.

As I mentioned earlier, you will not get any extra link juice from Twitter links since Twitter automatically places "no-follow" tags on Twitter links. You will, however, still get human visitors, so there is still a lot of upside if you can get the right kind of followers for your Tweets. Doing so, however, requires time and commitment—as all of these kinds of social marketing do.

YouTube, Flicker and Other Content Media Sharing Sites: For any site where you are allowed to post visual and audio media, from podcasts to video tutorials, it is always a good idea to tag your postings in a keyword savvy manner. These videos will work just like the images on your website. They will draw the search engines, especially when people are doing an image or video search on Google.

In addition, when creating podcasts, it is also a good idea to create written transcripts of your podcasts. If you have keyword optimized your podcast, the podcast transcript, which often has its own web page can work like a separate webpage, thus drawing traffic and allowing you to link back to your other sites, drawing traffic and link juice.

Final Conclusion

Finally, as we wrap up our discussion of SEO, I would like to emphasize that almost no two SEO campaigns are exactly alike. Although most of the steps are the same, a company's individual goals will alter the manner in which these steps are taken. Thus if you own a Real Estate site in Burbank, California, this will dictate a slightly different strategy than if you are trying to sell a Pizza Recipe Book online. In the first case, for example, much of the strategy will revolve around geo-targeting potential buyers interested in buying a home in Burbank, while location will be of much less importance for selling the pizza recipe book, since your readers will not be as geographically focused.

In the same way, the sites that get chosen for link back will be very different as well, since you want them to be topic specific in order to not get accused of improper methods of link-building. So you should not have a bunch of links to your Burbank real-estate business from an Iowa agriculture discussion board, for example.

So a proper and effective SEO campaign needs to retain a clear sense of a particular site's goals and expectations in order to be properly carried out. And, of course, as you may be aware by now, it takes a lot of time and consistent effort to properly conduct an SEO campaign. For professionals like me, it means setting up a client's website, automating as much of the process as possible, and doing the long hard work of site promotion one step at a time. If you know the ins and outs of the process as I do, you can save a lot of time and effort. If you are just learning the process, there will inevitably be a lot of trial and error.

If you set your mind to it, allot the time, and commit to it, you can do the SEO in-house. If you would rather just run your business and have as little head-ache as possible, then it is much easier and more efficient to let an SEO veteran like me do it for you.

Regardless of which you decide to do, I wish you good luck and lots of conversion ready traffic.

www.ingramcontent.com/pod-product-compliance
Lightning Source LLC
Chambersburg PA
CBHW080823170526
45158CB00009B/2511